THE MUSCULAR SYSTEM

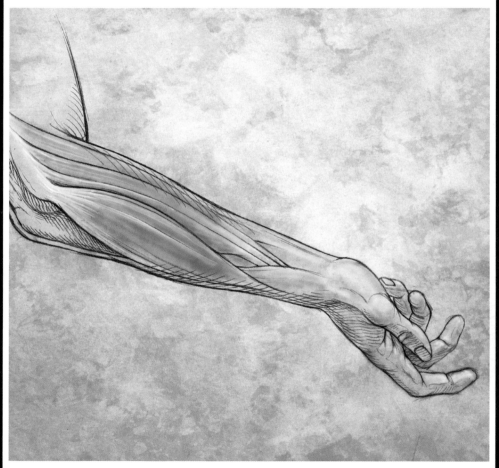

By Susan H. Gray

THE CHILD'S WORLD®
CHANHASSEN, MINNESOTA

Published in the United States of America by the Child's World®
P.O. Box 326, Chanhassen, MN 55317-0326
800-599-READ
www.childsworld.com

Subject adviser:
R. John Solaro, Ph.D.,
Distinguished
University Professor
and Head, Department
of Physiology and
Biophysics, University
of Illinois Chicago,
Chicago, Illinois

Photo Credits: Cover: Artville/Scott Bodell; Corbis:, 7 and 8 (Lester V. Bergman), 9 (Patrik Giardino), 15 (Kim Robbie), 18 (Jose Luiz Pelaez), 20, 21 (Science Pictures Limited), 27 (David H. Wells); Custom Medical Stock Pictures: 10, 11, 12, 13, 14, 16, 17, 19, 22, 26; PhotoEdit 5 and 6 (Tom Prettyman), 22 and 25, (Michael Newman), 24 (Felicia Martinez).

The Child's World®: Mary Berendes, Publishing Director

Editorial Directions, Inc.: E. Russell Primm, Editorial Director; Elizabeth K. Martin, Line Editor; Katie Marsico, Assistant Editor; Olivia Nellums, Editorial Assistant; Susan Hindman, Copy Editor; Elizabeth K. Martin, Proofreader; Peter Garnham, Marilyn Mallin, Mary Hoffman, Fact Checkers; Tim Griffin/IndexServ, Indexer; Cian Loughlin O'Day, Photo Researcher; Linda S. Koutris, Photo Selector

Library of Congress Cataloging-in-Publication Data
Gray, Susan Heinrichs.
  The muscular system / by Susan H. Gray.
    p. cm. — (Living well)
Includes bibliographical references and index.
Contents: What is the muscular system?—What are the parts of a muscle?—How can muscles make you move?—What makes a muscle contract?—Healthy and unhealthy muscles.
  ISBN 1-59296-038-3 (lib. bdg. : alk. paper)
  1. Muscles—Juvenile literature. [1. Muscular system. 2. Muscles.] I. Title. II. Series: Living well (Child's World (Firm)
  QP321.G76 2004
  612.7'4—dc21   2003006290

TABLE OF CONTENTS

CHAPTER ONE

JEREMY PROVES HIMSELF

"Hey, Jeremy! Show us your muscles!" Jeremy's big brothers were showing off. Each one was trying to prove how strong he was. One brother dropped to the ground and did six push-ups. The other one jumped up and grabbed a tree limb with one hand. He slowly pulled himself up and touched his chin to the limb.

Jeremy shouted back, "Watch this!" He ran over to a concrete block at the corner of the playground. He squatted down and dug his fingertips under it. With his fingers under the block, Jeremy tried to stand up. His body grew tense. Electrical signals shot through his nerves. A special chemical flowed out of the nerves going to his muscle cells. The chemical made thousands of Jeremy's muscle cells try to shorten. Jeremy slowly rose, with the block still in his hands. More of

As Jeremy lifted the cement block, chemicals were shooting from his nerves to his muscles, telling them to shorten.

the chemical came out of his nerve endings. More muscle cells short-

ened. Jeremy stood up straight. Still more of the chemical flowed and

more cells went to work. Jeremy lifted the block up to his chest. His

Jeremy's muscular system came through for him as he showed off for his brothers.

arm muscles were bulging. His legs were trembling. Then he dropped

the block on the ground.

"Not bad, little guy!" Jeremy's brothers were impressed. Jeremy

didn't answer. He was breathing too heavily to talk. His legs and arms

were hurting. He had no energy left. However, he knew one thing. He

had certainly shown them his muscles.

CHAPTER TWO

WHAT IS THE MUSCULAR SYSTEM?

Throughout the body, there are three kinds of muscle tissue. Smooth muscle lies inside the walls of blood vessels and some of the organs. The heart is made of **cardiac** (KAR-dee-ak) muscles. **Skeletal** muscles are the ones we usually think of as muscles. They are in the arms and legs. They are in the back, front, neck, and face. These muscles help us move. They also help us sit and stand without falling over. Skeletal muscles make up the muscular system.

Sometimes skeletal muscles go by other names. They are often called striated (STRY-ate-ed) muscles. Striations (stry-AY-shuns) are little

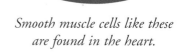

Smooth muscle cells like these are found in the heart.

stripes. Under a microscope, skeletal muscle appears to have many striations. Skeletal muscles are also called voluntary (VOLL-un-tehr-ee) muscles. If something is voluntary, that means we decide to do it ourselves. We have control. We can control the movements of voluntary muscles. Involuntary muscles work without us telling them to. The

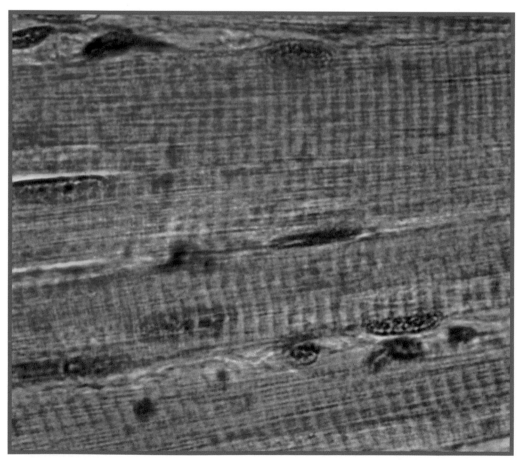

You can see the many striations, or stripes, on this microscopic view of a skeletal muscle.

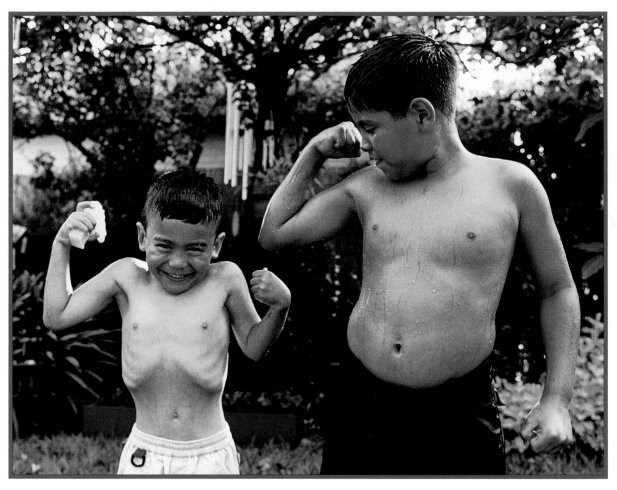

*Muscles in your arms can stretch, shorten, or return
to their normal size when you want them to.*

heart is a special kind of involuntary muscle. Other involuntary mus-

cles are found in the lungs and blood vessels.

All muscle tissue—no matter what kind it is—can do four things.

It can extend, or stretch. It contracts, or shortens. It can always return

to its normal size. Last, it reacts to things in its environment. In the

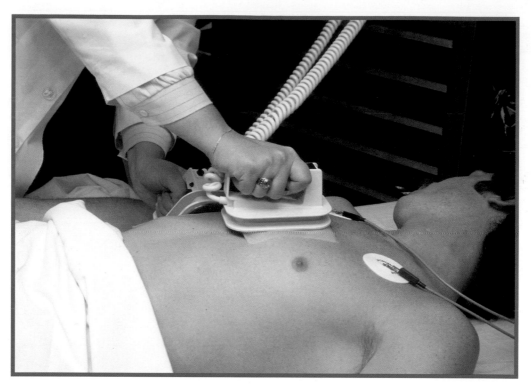

A doctor is giving this patient's heart muscle an electric shock to make it beat normally.

body, a muscle reacts to chemicals in its environment. The chemicals come from nerve tips and cause muscles to contract.

Muscles also react to electricity. Sometimes a person whose heart is not beating normally goes to the hospital. The doctor can give the heart muscle an electrical shock. If things work right, the heart reacts to the shock. It stops beating for just a moment. Then it starts beating normally.

Scientists have been interested in muscles for centuries. More than 2,000 years ago, the ancient Greek Aristotle studied animals. He watched their movements. Aristotle decided that people and animals moved because of breath flowing all through their bodies. He believed this breath went through the heart and out to the arms and legs.

Later, an ancient Roman named Galen studied human bodies. He was a doctor for the Roman gladiators. Galen decided that movement was not controlled by some special breath. It was controlled by the brain.

Over the next thousand years, scientists continued to study the body. In the late 1400s, Leonardo da Vinci got into the act. He was an artist and a scientist. He showed how muscles could make bones move. He drew pictures of actual muscles and bones to support his ideas.

A doctor named Andreas Vesalius made his own drawings (left). The drawings showed hundreds of muscles in the human body. Vesalius believed that something inside the muscle itself caused it to contract. Of course, he did not know about nerve chemicals.

Since Vesalius's time, scientists have learned much about nerve chemicals. They have even studied the tiny nerve endings and muscle cells under the microscope.

CHAPTER THREE

WHAT ARE THE PARTS
OF A MUSCLE?

Muscle is really the "meat" of the body. When you eat chicken, you are eating bird muscles. When you eat tuna, you are eating muscle tissue from the fish. In many animals, muscles form a large part of the body. In humans, they make up about one-third to one-half of a person's weight.

Voluntary muscles are loaded with blood vessels and nerves. Blood brings food and oxygen to muscles so they can work. Blood also takes away waste materials.

Muscles are made up of many tiny cells. Each cell is smaller in diameter than a human hair. However, cells can be several

The colored blobs in this picture are really groups of striated muscles coming together as muscle fibers.

feet long. Muscle cells are also called muscle fibers (FY-burz). Nerves run from the spinal cord out to the muscles. The spinal cord is a thick bundle of nerves running down the back. It connects the brain to the muscles. When the nerves reach the muscles, they split into many branches. Each branch comes to an end right on a muscle fiber.

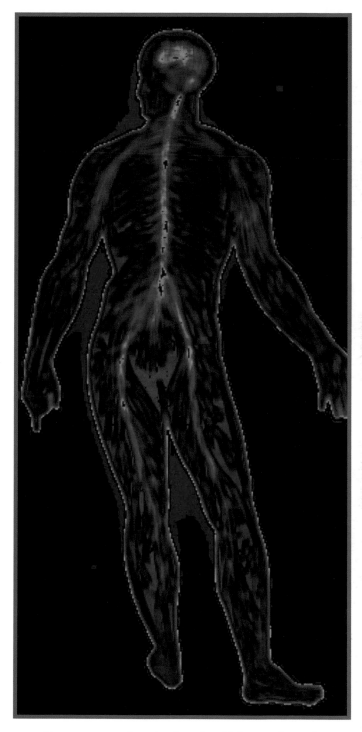

Nerves connect the spinal cord, which runs down the middle of your back, to the many muscles of your body.

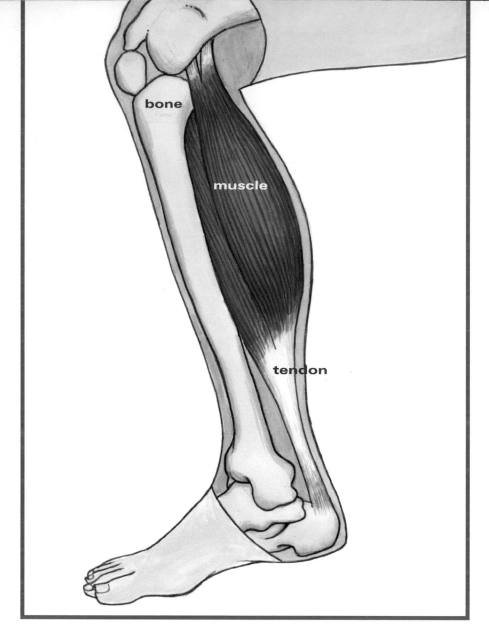

*Skeletal muscles are connected to bones. This leg muscle
is attached to the heel bone by the Achilles tendon.*

Skeletal muscles have at least two ends. One end is anchored to a

bone. The other end is attached to another bone or a tissue. The

tough cord that attaches a muscle to a bone is called a tendon.

Muscles have all kinds of shapes. Some of the muscles in the back are wide sheets of tissue. Circular muscles surround the eyes and mouth. When you pucker your lips, the circular muscle around your mouth contracts. When you close your eyes tightly, the circular muscles around your eyes go to work. Most muscles are in the shape of straps or bands. The muscles that make your eyes roll are such muscles.

Muscles shaped like bands make this girl's eyes roll. Circular muscles and straplike muscles help her mouth move.

CHAPTER FOUR

How Can Muscles Make You Move?

There are about 650 voluntary muscles in the body. They give the body its shape. They also help you move in every way you can imagine. Muscles in the hips, legs, feet, and toes help you to run. Muscles around the eyes make you squint. Muscles in the arm move your fingers. Muscles in the neck operate your tongue.

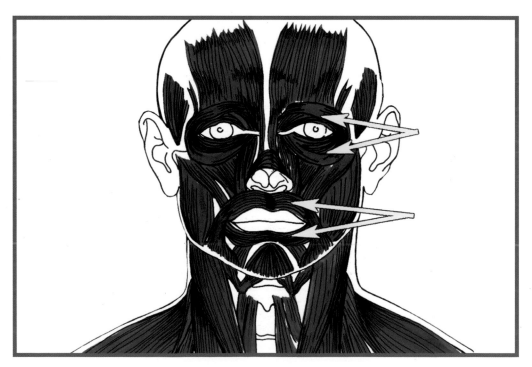

The muscles around your eyes and mouth make a goofy face possible!

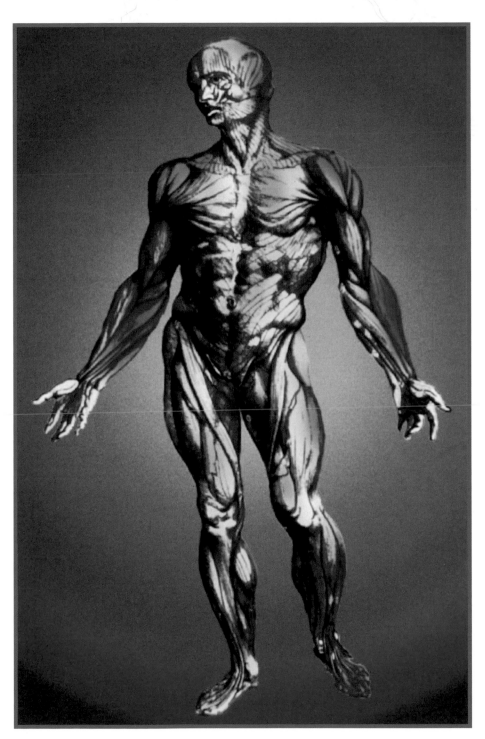

There are muscles just about everywhere in the human body.

The calf muscles of these dancers contract and harden to keep them on the tips of their toes.

You move because your muscles contract, or shorten. They develop a force or tension. When a muscle contracts, it pulls on a body part. When it pulls, that body part moves. Try this yourself. Point your foot down. Notice how your **calf** muscle contracts and hardens. When the muscle contracted, it pulled your heel bone up. Now point your foot up. To do this, the muscles on the front of your leg contract-ed. They pulled your foot up. You can even feel the muscles harden up as they do so.

You have just seen how muscles work in pairs. One muscle pulls a body part one way. Another muscle pulls it the opposite way. Muscles never push body parts—they always pull.

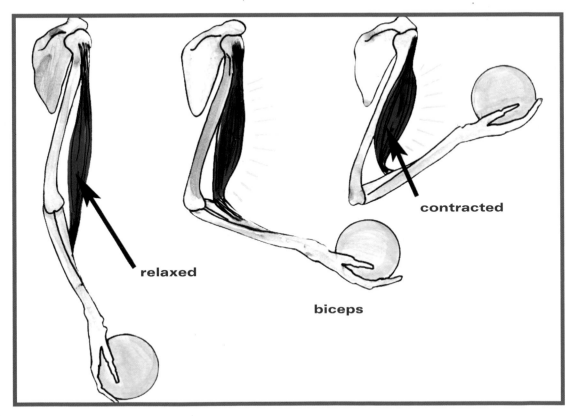

Upper arm muscles called biceps contract to help you lift an object.
Different arm muscles contract as you put that object down.

CHAPTER FIVE

WHAT MAKES A MUSCLE CONTRACT?

For a whole muscle to contract, many tiny muscle cells must contract at once. When it is time for a muscle to move, the nerve endings go into action. They release a special chemical. The chemical causes the fibers to contract. When many, many fibers contract at once, the whole muscle contracts. Lifting a feather only activates a few muscle cells. Lifting a heavy backpack activates many more cells.

When it is time for a muscle to relax, another chemical comes along. It stops the action of the first chemical. This allows the fibers to relax and return to their normal size.

Nerves need to activate more muscle cells to help you pick up a backpack than a feather.

Nerve endings connect to striated muscles, releasing chemicals that make the muscles move.

Just imagine what happens every time you move. Millions of

nerve endings put out chemicals. The chemicals make millions of tiny

fibers contract. All of those little contractions make whole muscles

contract. The muscles pull on body parts to make them move.

Have you ever heard of tetanus (TET-n-us) shots? Have you ever wondered what they are? You probably got the shots when you were a baby. These are shots that keep you from getting a terrible disease called tetanus. The germs that cause the disease live in the dirt. If a person gets a deep wound and dirt gets in, the germs might also get in. Once inside the body, the germ cells multiply. Each germ cell puts out a deadly poison. Within days, the germs spread throughout the whole body. They release more and more poison. The person begins to feel sick. Neck and face muscles become tense.

The person is said to have lockjaw.

In time, more muscles tense up. They contract but can't relax. Some muscles may tremble or shake wildly. By then, the poison is everywhere in the body. How does it cause all of these problems? The poison works on the nerve chemicals. It won't let the chemicals work normally. The poison keeps the muscles from relaxing, so all the muscles contract at once. This causes a person to become very tense and rigid. The person cannot swallow. People have died from this disease. The best way to avoid it is to get those tetanus shots.

NDC 49281-271-83
Tetanus and Diphtheria Toxoids Adsorbed For Adult Use
5 mL
R only

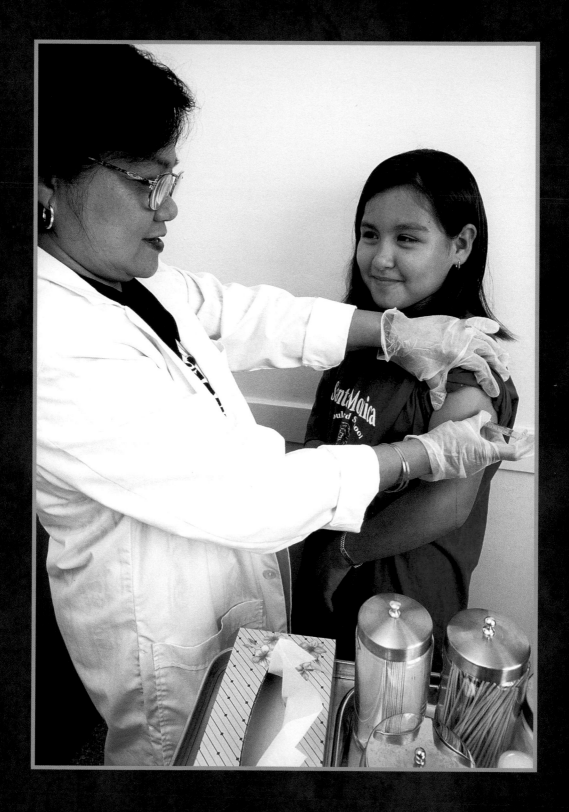

CHAPTER SIX

HEALTHY AND UNHEALTHY MUSCLES

T he muscular system keeps you moving. That is why

everyone should try to keep it healthy. A healthy muscu-

lar system needs plenty of water and the right foods. High-protein

foods help build and repair muscle tissue. Such foods include eggs,

milk, meat, fish, and nuts.

Proteins found in foods such as these help to build healthy muscles.

Cereal and breads contain carbohydrates that give muscles energy.

For energy, muscles need **carbohydrates.** Bread, cereal, crackers, and potatoes contain these. Calcium and potassium are important for nerves to work properly. They also keep muscles from cramping. Calcium is in milk, cheese, and yogurt. Potassium is in bananas.

Sometimes, the muscular system can become diseased. Even with proper nutrition, the muscles might not get better. Muscular dystrophy (DISS-truh-fee) is one such disease. Over time, the muscles become weaker and less able to function. Myasthenia gravis (MY-us-THEEN-ee-uh GRAV-iss) is another muscular disease. Here, the body will not let the nerve chemicals do their job. Muscles cannot contract properly. A person with this disease might have trouble talking, swallowing, or moving.

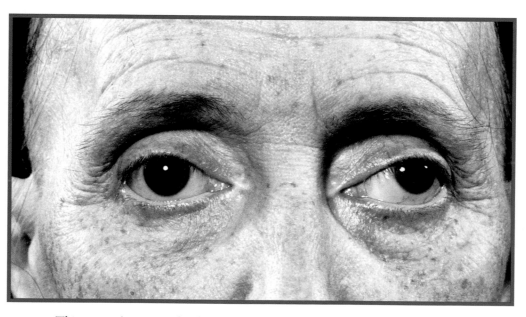

This patient's eye muscles do not move correctly because of myasthenia gravis.

Exercise can be fun and keeps your muscular system healthy.

Scientists are looking at how healthy and diseased muscles work. They are studying the nerve chemicals. They are looking at the molecules deep inside muscle fibers. Scientists are looking at how damaged muscle repairs itself. They are learning more about how exercise and diet affect muscles. We have come a long way since the days of Aristotle. However, there is still plenty to learn.

Glossary

calf (KAF) The muscle in the back part of the lower leg is the calf.

carbohydrates (KAR-bo-HY-drates) Carbohydrates are types of food that are built out of sugars.

cardiac (KAR-dee-ak) Cardiac means having to do with the heart.

skeletal (SKELL-uh-tul) Something that is skeletal has to do with the skeleton.

Questions and Answers about the Muscular System

If I exercise, can I turn fat cells into muscle cells? No, fat cells will always be fat cells. But with exercise, you can build up your muscle cells while fat cells shrink in size.

Which muscles control my fingers? Most of the muscles that control your finger movements are not in your fingers. They are in your lower arm. These muscles have very long tendons that run out to the finger bones.

Sometimes I get cramps in my leg and foot muscles. Why does this happen? Many things could cause your muscles to cramp, and this can be very painful. Often, when people do not get enough calcium or potassium in their diets, their muscles will cramp. A blood clot in the leg might also cause cramping when it keeps blood from reaching the muscle.

Did You Know?

- When people feel cold, they shiver. This is a muscle activity that produces heat. It is a way that muscles work to keep the body warm.

- Vesalius, a 16th-century doctor, studied the body by dissecting people who had died. Many of his subjects were prisoners who had been condemned to death.

- The smallest skeletal muscle in the human body is inside the ear. It is smaller than a rice grain, and it moves a tiny bone that helps you to hear.

- Some people believe that exercise turns fat cells into muscle cells. This is not true. Exercise builds up the muscle cells. Fat cells always remain fat cells.

- When you get goose bumps, the hairs on your arm stand up. These hairs stand up because tiny muscles are attached to their roots and pull on them.

How to Learn More about the Muscular System

At the Library

Avila, Victoria, and Antonio Muñoz Parramon.
How Our Muscles Work.
New York: Chelsea House Publishers, 1995.

Ballard, Carol, and Steve Parker.
The Skeleton and Muscular System.
Austin, Tex.: Raintree/Steck-Vaughn, 1997.

Silverstein, Alvin, Virginia Silverstein, and Robert Silverstein.
The Muscular System.
New York: Twenty-First Century Books, 1994.

On the Web

Visit our home page for lots of links about muscles:
http://www.childsworld.com/links.html
Note to Parents, Teachers, and Librarians: We routinely verify our
Web links to make sure they're safe, active sites—so encourage
your readers to check them out!

Through the Mail or by Phone

MUSCULAR DYSTROPHY ASSOCIATION
National Headquarters
3300 E. Sunrise Drive
Tucson, AZ 85718
800-572-1717
http://www.mdausa.org

NATIONAL INSTITUTE OF ARTHRITIS AND
MUSCULOSKELETAL AND SKIN DISEASES
Information Clearinghouse
National Institutes of Health
1 AMS Circle
Bethesda, Maryland 20892-3675
301-495-4484
http://www.niams.nih.gov

Index

About the Author

Susan H. Gray has a bachelor's and a master's degree in zoology, and has taught college-level anatomy and physiology courses. In her 25 years as an author, she has written many medical articles, grant proposals, and children's books. Ms. Gray enjoys gardening, traveling, and playing the piano and organ. She has traveled twice to the Russian Far East to give organ workshops to church musicians. She also works extensively with American and Russian friends to develop medical and social service programs for Vladivostok, Russia. Ms. Gray and her husband, Michael, live in Cabot, Arkansas.